About the Book

There are whole communities of plants and animals living in small spaces that we usually overlook. Ferns, moss and lichen, ants, spiders and crickets may be found hidden away under rocks, in wall cracks or other out of the way places. Here, sheltered from the weather and other animals they thrive in their own tiny environment.

Wilda Ross' informative text and Arabelle Wheatley's colorful illustrations help us peek into unexpected places to discover the wonders of a miniature world all around us.

cracks and crannies what lives there

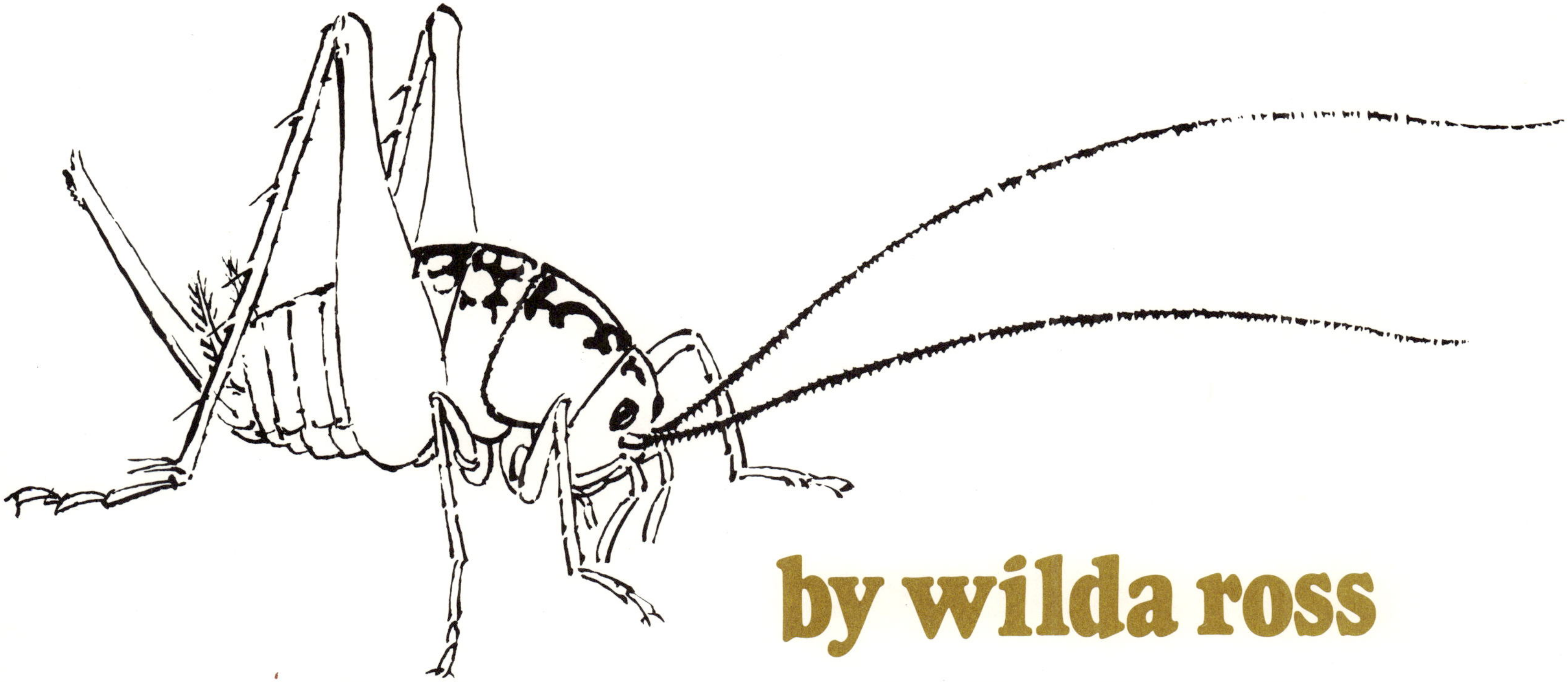

by wilda ross

illustrated by arabelle wheatley

COWARD, McCANN & GEOGHEGAN, INC. NEW YORK

General Editor: Margaret Farrington Bartlett

 Published simultaneously in Canada by Longman Canada Limited, Toronto.

SBN: GB-698-30598-1
SBN: TR-698-20346-1

Library of Congress Catalog Card Number: 75-7528

PRINTED IN THE UNITED STATES OF AMERICA
07211

To Alex

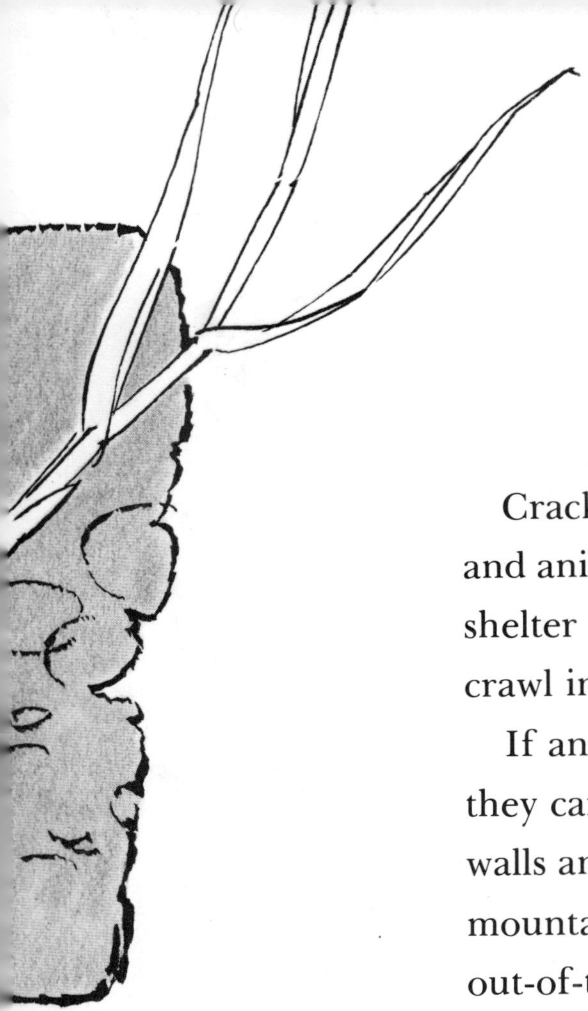

Cracks and crannies are leftover places where some plants and animals manage to live and even flourish. Here they find shelter from the weather, as well as from animals too large to crawl in after them.

If animals are small and flat enough like ants and worms, they can live in sidewalk cracks and chinks between rocks in walls and buildings. Outside cities, in grasslands, forests, and mountains, whole communities of plants and animals live in out-of-the-way places such as soil cracks, under stones or the barks of trees, between huge boulders on mountainsides.

Plants with flyaway seeds like grasses and daisies often grow in sidewalk cracks. How many kinds of plants can you find growing in sidewalk cracks? City plants, like city people, often come from faraway places.

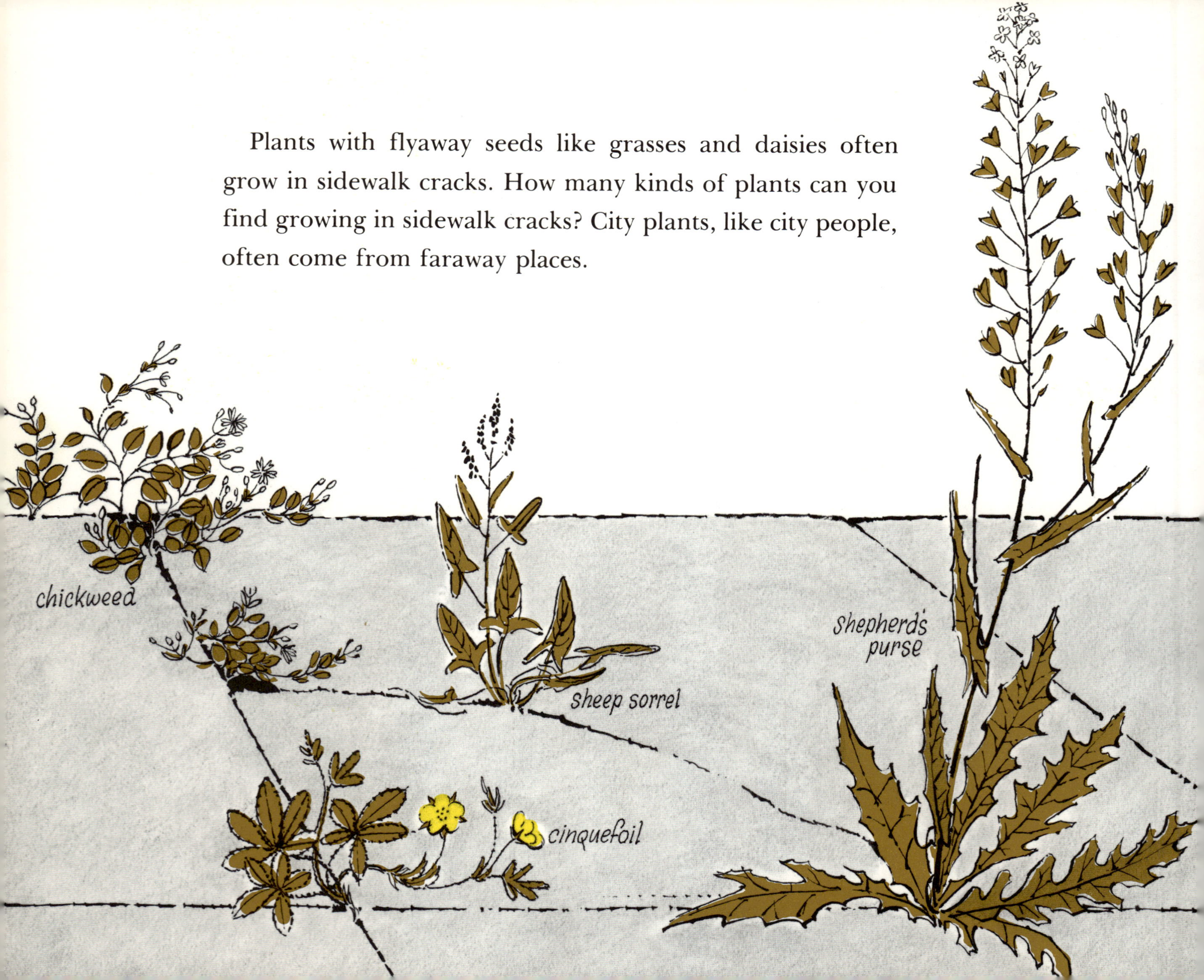

ox-eye daisy
broad-leaved plantain
quack grass
Knot-grass
yellow wood sorrel

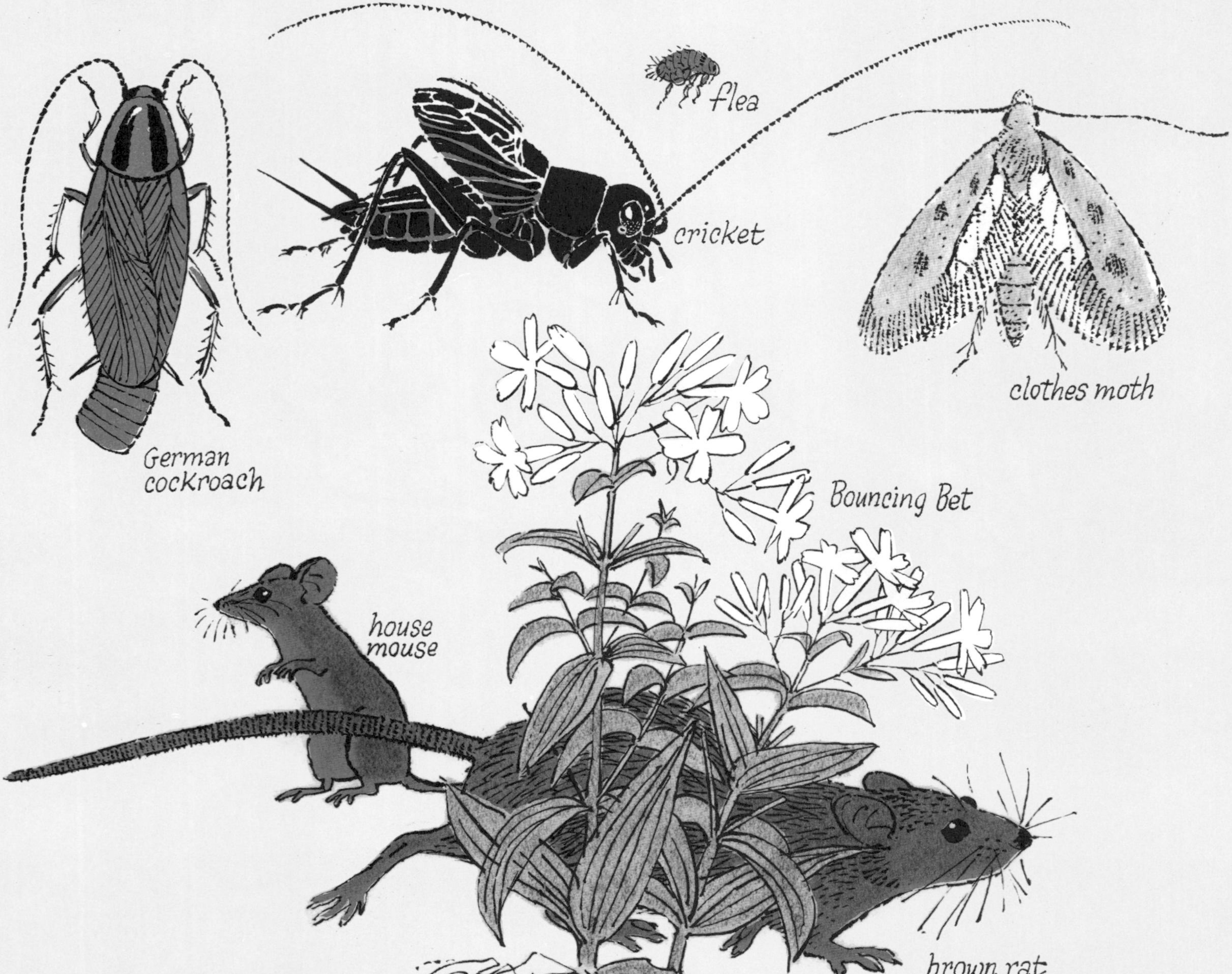

flea
cricket
German cockroach
clothes moth
Bouncing Bet
house mouse
brown rat

The first settlers to come from Europe brought seeds to plant for food. These seeds were mixed with the wild plant seeds that usually grow in fields. Also coming along with the settlers in their clothing and household furnishings were clothes moths, cockroaches, crickets, fleas, rats, and mice. They all continued to live together in the cracks and crannies around our homes and gardens. When cities were gradually built over the farmlands, some of the stowaways remained in the cities.

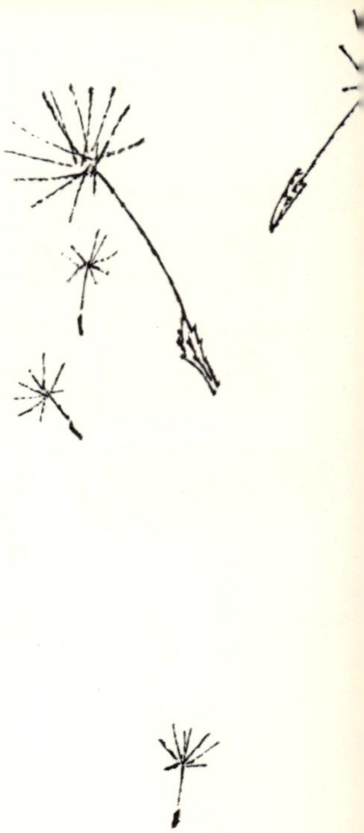

So many dandelions grow in sidewalk cracks because their parachute seeds are easily carried on the wind. Each dandelion flower produces so many seeds that some will certainly land in the pockets of soil that collect between buildings and street cracks.

dandelion

Garden walls have lots of cracks and crannies where animals and plants can live. Tiny brown Argentine ants raise large families between the rocks in the wall. They will eat other insects they meet by chance, but their favorite foods are in your kitchen.

Ant scouts fan out in all directions from a nest in search of food. How does the ant find its way home? Whenever an ant goes out of the nest, it marks the trail with droplets of fluid containing its own special odor. With sensitive antennae touching the ground, the ant can pick up its own scent or that of the nest mates and thus follow the trail to its home. Soon long black columns of ants are streaming along the shortest path to your kitchen.

Sow bugs also hide in rock walls as far from an ant colony as possible because ants will attack a sow bug in great numbers and pull it to pieces—that is, unless the sow bug can roll up into a ball first. These crusty crawlers come out of their hiding places on cool mornings to feed on rotting leaves and young tender plants. They like moist crevices because they breathe through gills like fish. Indeed crabs, lobsters, and shrimp are also members of their group.

Centipedes live in the dark cool shelter of chinks in foundations and rock walls. These animal boxcars with a pair of legs for each body section or segment slither out at night to hunt cockroaches, clothes moths, and other insects. They too are crusty like sow bugs but have many more segments and pairs of legs.

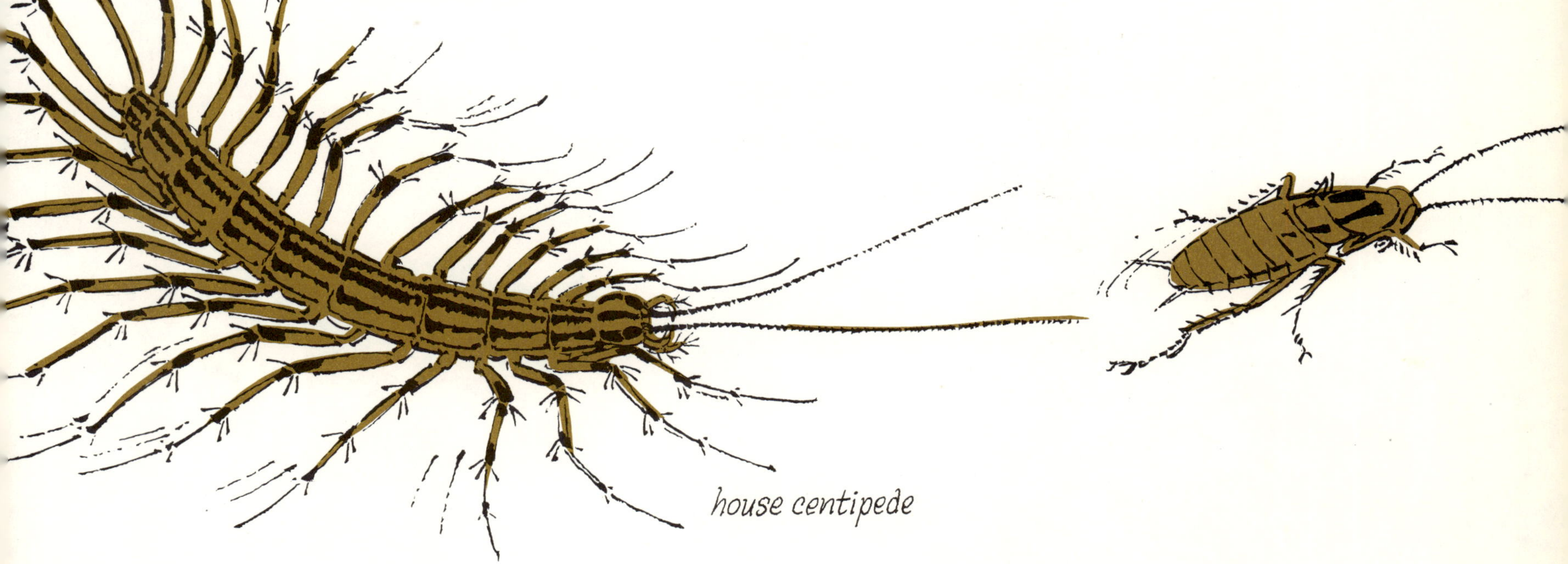

house centipede

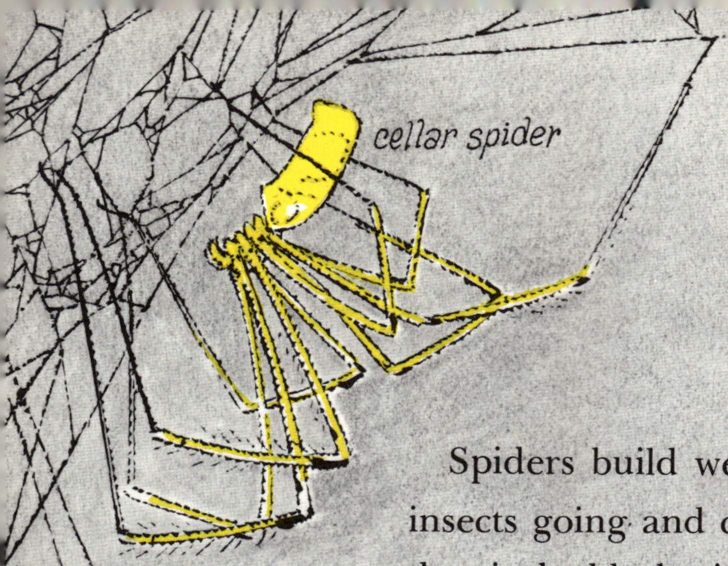

Spiders build webs over nooks and crannies to catch the insects going and coming there. Most poisonous of city spiders is the black widow that lives in garden walls, houses, and barns. This shiny black spider with the red hourglass on its abdomen constructs a tunnel-shaped web to trap unwary insects. The spider waits at the bottom of the tunnel for the slightest movement on the web which might mean that food is there for the taking.

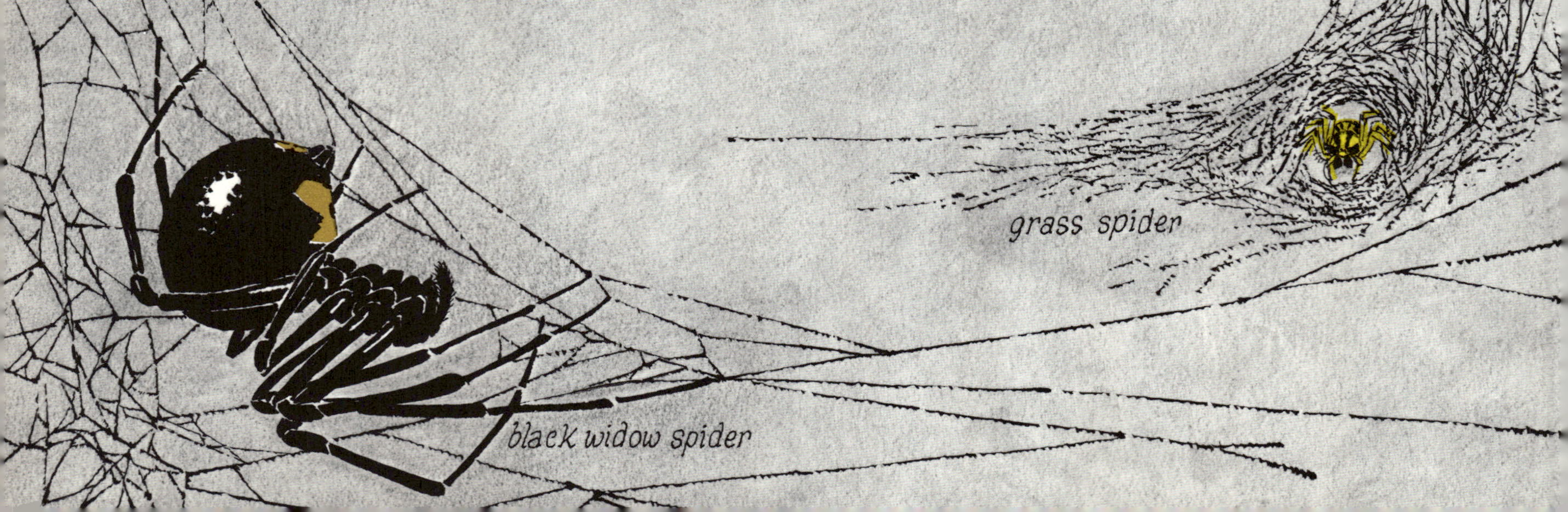

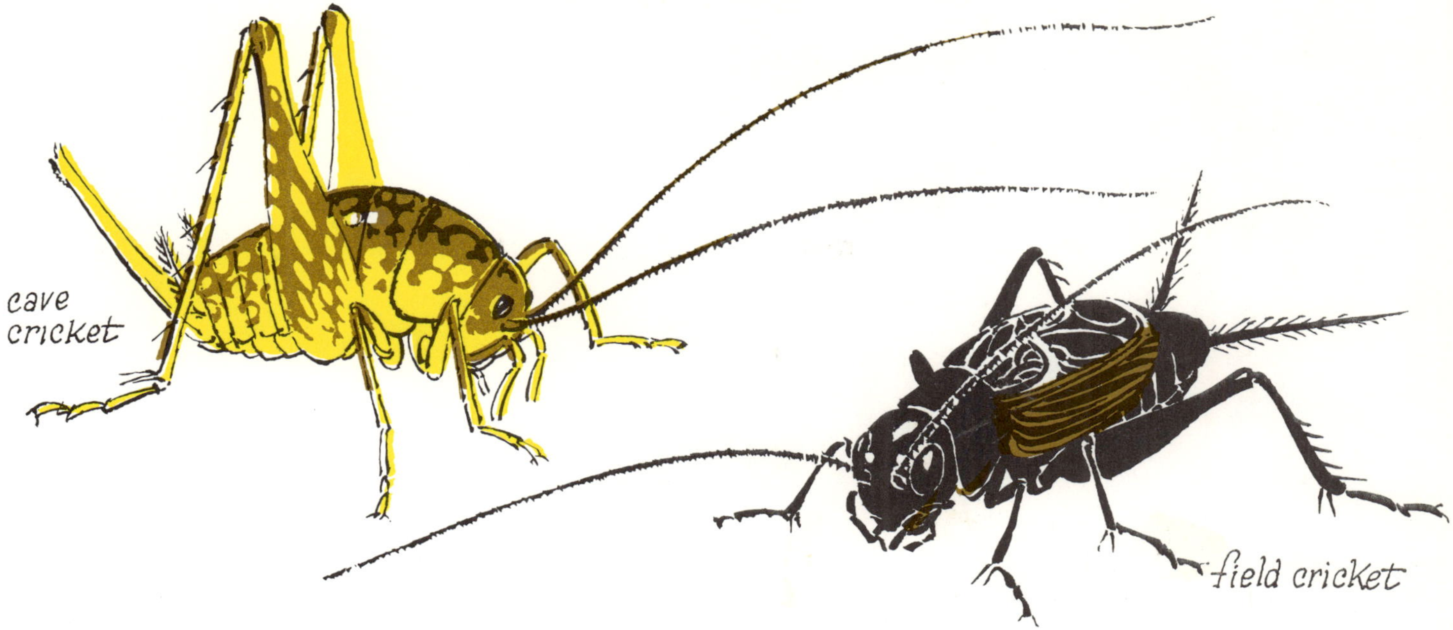

Crickets were already living in the cracks of cave walls, eating the leftover scraps from animal diners, when people moved in. When we moved from the caves, some crickets came along with us. They have been living in and around our houses ever since. We brought some to North America, and many were already here, always hiding in dark places during the daytime, coming out to feed at night.

polypody fern
hair-cap mosses
slug
sphagnum moss
spleenwort fern
feather moss

Ferns and mosses grow well on garden walls, where their roots can remain cool and moist. This is also a place for snails and slugs to hide during the heat of the day, crawling out on cool mornings to eat tender plants in your garden. We also brought a snail from Europe which is more common than the ones that were already here.

The European brown snail, as it is commonly known, glides forth on a ribbon of slime which comes from an opening just beneath the mouth. The slime helps keep it moist. Snails can travel as fast as two inches a minute. A cluster of pearly eggs is laid under a stone or clod of soil in early spring. The babies grow all summer and reach the size of plump chestnuts by fall.

European brown snail

House or English sparrows are the commonest birds in all our towns and cities. They build their ragged nests of string and grass in the eaves of houses or any small hole in a building where they can find shelter from wind and rain.

English sparrows are not really English at all. They were living in North African cities a very long time before they arrived in England. Early settlers brought a few pairs of these chirpy, chunky birds to the United States with hopes they would eat insect pests. In fact, they prefer picnic leftovers, seeds, and tender plants.

PIZ

In some places, like high mountains, cracks and crannies are often the best places to live. Overhanging boulders protect seedlings from wind and throw heat back off their sun-warmed surfaces. Snow catches between the rocks in winter and forms a protecting blanket. Almost all the spaces between the rocks are possible homes.

High mountains are made of hard rocks. Earthquakes and volcanic eruptions crack rocks instantly. Changes in temperature and winds crack them more slowly. Even plants crack rocks.

Lichens are the first plants to grow on bare rocks. Their pale green, gray, orange, or yellow circles often cover the rocks. Two kinds of plants living together make up a lichen. One is a green alga which makes food from sunlight, minerals in the rocks, and water. The other plant is a fungus growing in long cottonlike fibers around the algae. Both kinds of plants live elsewhere separately. Algae live commonly as green scum on pond water. Fungi are better known as mushrooms.

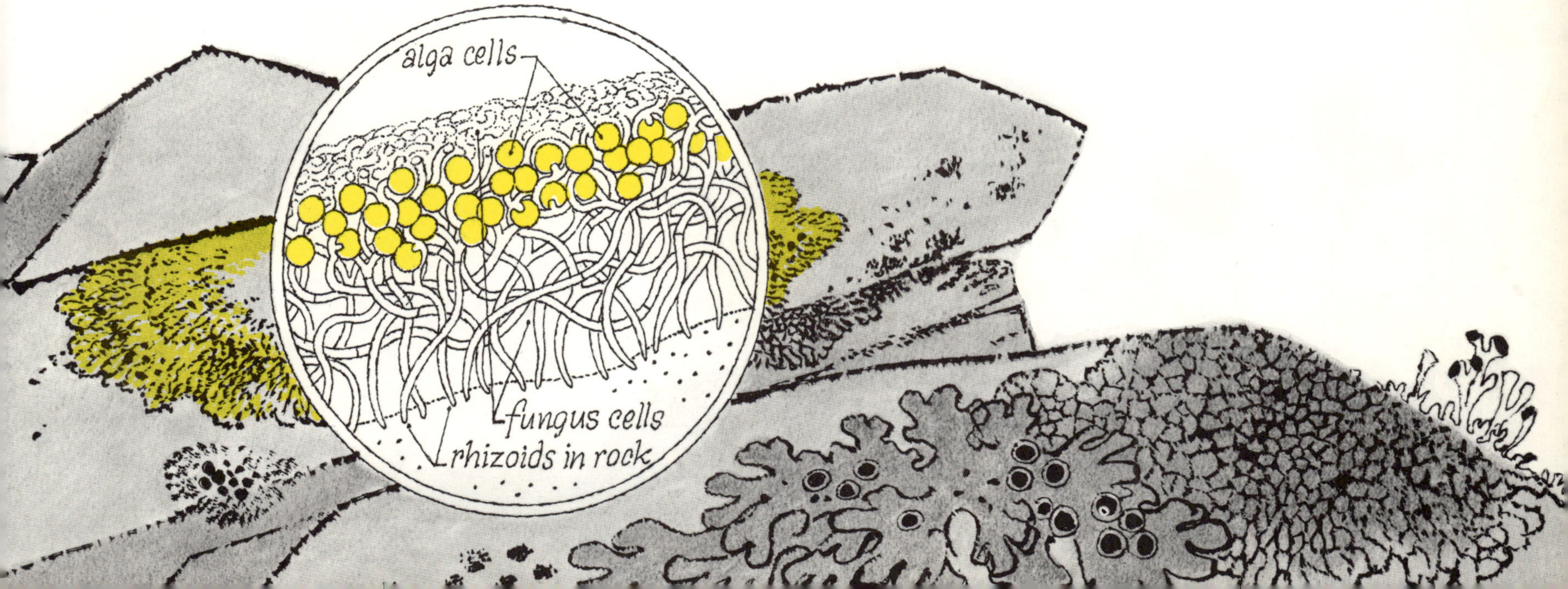

Hairlike fibers, called rhizomes, fasten lichens to the rocks. Acids in the lichens slowly dissolve bits of rock. Small cavities develop on the smooth surfaces. Like a footpath on a hill, once the wearing process begins, it goes faster and faster to make a groove. Mosses and ferns quicken the process. Bits of rotting plants collect to make pockets of soil where a few hardy flowers and shrubs eventually take root.

The plants that do manage to live in high mountain cracks and crannies have special forms in addition to being small and flat. Plants are shorter, thinner, less branched, and with fewer flowers on a stem. Generally the flowers are large in proportion to the plant because seed production is their most important job.

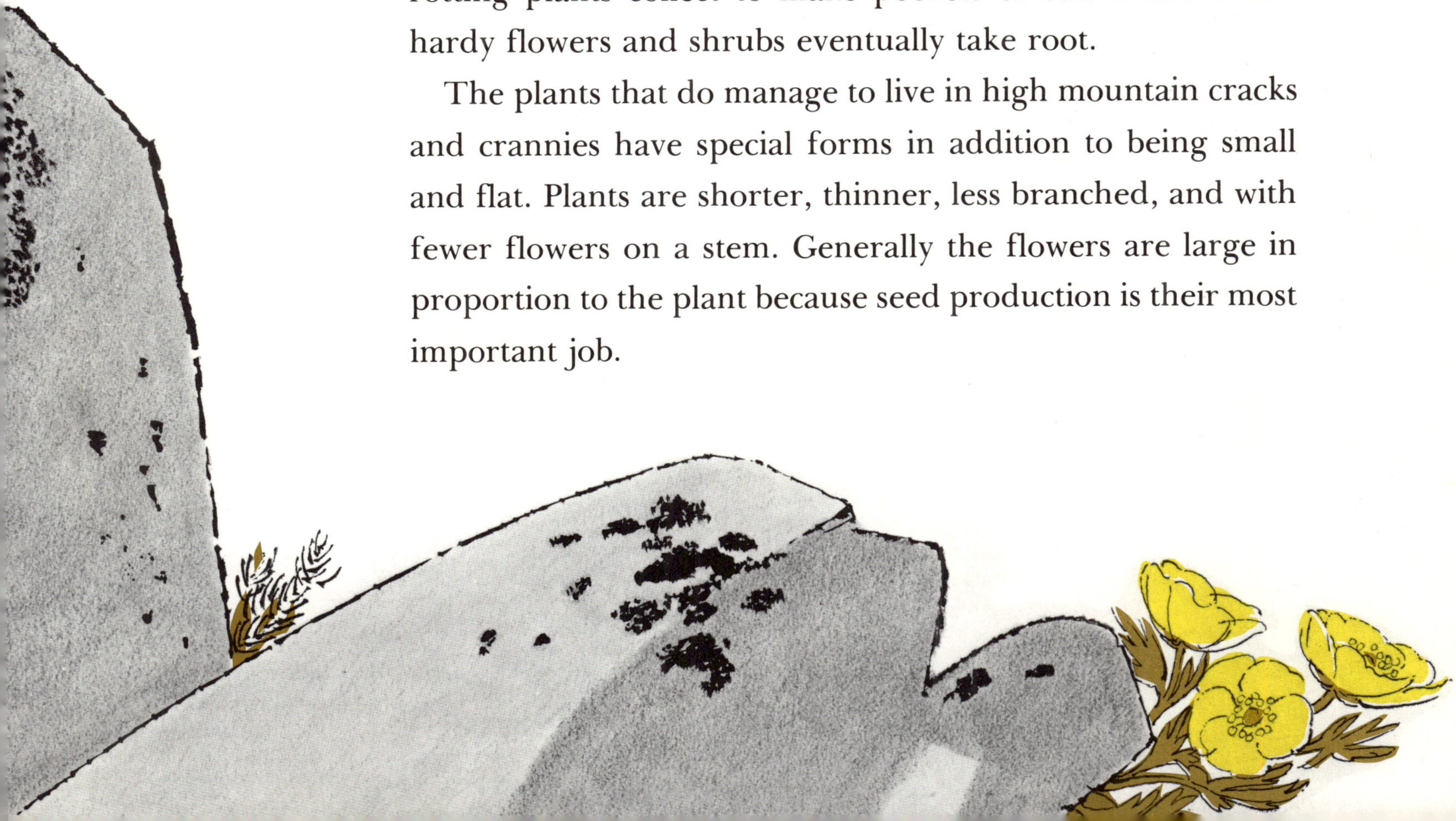

Of all the plants taking advantage of these pockets of soil, grasses and sedges are the most numerous. Their narrow leaves bend easily with the strong winds. Flowers are enclosed in protecting envelopes.

Most spaces between rocks are narrow. Animals living there have to be small. Food is scarce. There is not enough for large families. The one or two babies must grow up fast during the short warm season when food is most abundant. Ants tunnel their nests around the grass roots, hunting beetle larvae that feed there. Black wolf spiders, crab spiders, and orb weaver spiders hunt the ants and a few butterflies that come up the mountain in summer.

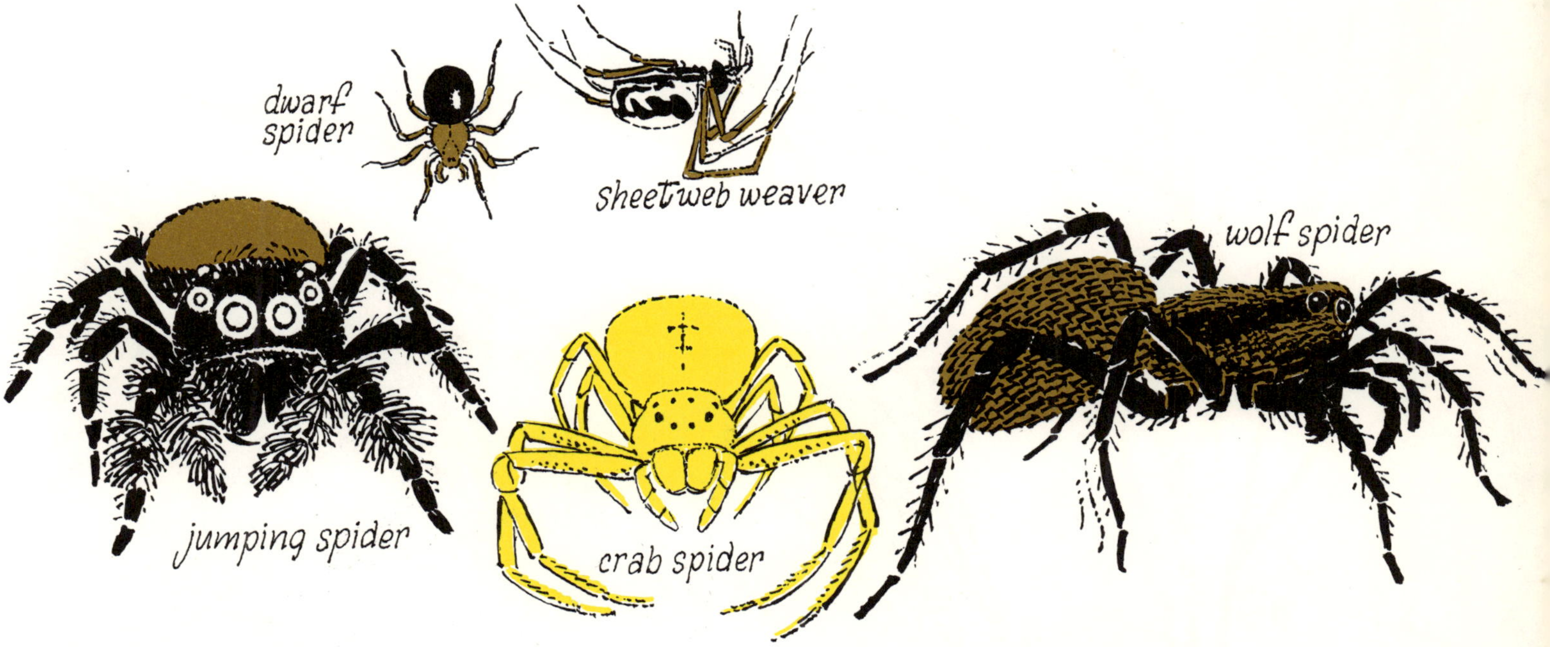

Guinea-pig-sized animals, called pikas, dart about carrying pieces of grass, which they pile in neat stacks on sunny boulders. When the hay is dry, the pika stores it under an overhanging rock for a winter food supply.

Marmots are baggy teddy bear cousins of squirrels that sleep all winter in cozy crevices. They spend the short summer eating plants and putting on fat almost equal to half their body weight. Like squirrels, marmots have begging ways and are not a bit shy of summer hikers.

yellowbelly marmot

We still have lots to learn about the creatures living in out-of-the-way places around us. Now that you know more about the lives of your hidden neighbors, perhaps you can discover more secrets of how they manage to survive.

Think of all the out-of-the-way places in between mountains and cities: tree holes in forest and orchard, cracks in tree bark, cracks in dry soil on farms and open plains.

No matter where you are, you can be sure a small plant or animal has a home. How many of these homes can you find in the cracks and crannies around you?

About the Author

Wilda Ross has always been fascinated by plants and animals. At the University of California at Berkeley she took her degree in botany. She has initiated and directed natural history programs, studied and collected ants, worked for the Bureau of Insect Identification of the U.S. Department of Agriculture and taught classes in natural history.

She enjoys writing science books for children. Among her books are WHO LIVES IN THIS LOG?, WHAT DID DINOSAURS EAT? and CAN YOU FIND THE ANIMAL? all written for Coward, McCann & Geoghegan.

Wilda Ross lives in Mill Valley, California.

About the Artist

Arabelle Wheatley is a graduate of the Art Institute of Pittsburgh. She worked as an artist in the advertising field until, she says, she realized how much fun illustrating books was. Mrs. Wheatley has illustrated more than nine books for children and did all the plant and animal drawings for the Encyclopedia International.

Ms. Wheatley and her husband live in Florida. Recently, they bought an old farm house in Pennsylvania that they're busy renovating. They plan to spend their summers in it when it's finished.